RENE'S BOUQUETS™

René van Rems AIFD

RENE'S

A GUIDE TO EURO-STYLE

BOUQUETS™

HAND-TIED BOUQUETS

RENE VAN REMS INTERNATIONAL

FLORAL DESIGN|ART DIRECTION: René van Rems AIFD

PROJECT MANAGEMENT: Randy R. Marks

EDITOR: Bruce Wright

SPANISH TRANSLATION: María Dolores Bolívar

DESIGN AND COMPOSITION: Kaelin Chappell Broaddus

WEB DEVELOPMENT: Matt Young, Objective A Development

STYLIST: Erin Mcdonald

ASSISTANT TO MR. VAN REMS: Heidi R. Hamann

PHOTOGRAPHERS:

Al Quiala for Pacific+, Carlsbad, California, pages 4, 8, 10, 16, 18, 22, 30, 40, 43, 48–78, 20–129;

Gary Conaughton, pages 12–14, 20, 24, 26–28, 32, 36–37, 39, 42, 44–45, 47, 79;

photos on pages 33–35 appear courtesy of Pokon Chrysal

COVER PHOTOGRAPHER: Al Quiala for Pacific+

PREPRESS PRODUCTION: Pacific+ and Partner Press

PRINTER: Doosan Printing, South Korea

To request permission to make copies of any part of the work please call René van Rems International at:
1-888-824-7363

www.renevanrems.com

ISBN-10: 0-9770245-0-4

Printed in South Korea
Second edition 2007
K J I H G F E D C B A

ACKNOWLEDGMENTS
AGRADECIMIENTOS

The Netherlands, or Holland as some know the country, is renowned as "the flower capital of the world." So it comes as no surprise that I was exposed to the love of flowers at an early age. Artists and designers have always taken inspiration from flowers and plants. But in the Netherlands it's understood that flowers can themselves be an artistic medium. Living in a flat in Amsterdam, we had no garden other than a few planters on the balcony. But I will always remember the enthusiasm and pride with which my mother created and maintained those planters. They were the talk of the neighborhood!

I owe the nurturing of my creativity and my passion for the visual arts to both my mother and my father. My mother was involved in the haute couture industry, my father in the world of vintage automobiles, both decidedly visual enterprises. They always supported my "playing with flowers" and encouraged me to take my first floral arranging course with my (future) mentor Abel Verheijen.

I am grateful to have studied with Abel under the old European system of apprenticeship, which today has virtually disappeared. He took me under his tutelage at age 13 and showed me the flower world of

Los países bajos u Holanda, como algunos conocen al país, gozan del renombre de ser "capital mundial de las flores". No sorprende el que haya estado expuesto al amor por las flores desde temprana edad. Los artistas y diseñadores se han inspirado siempre en flores y plantas. Pero en Holanda se entiende que las flores sean, en sí mismas, instrumento del arte. Al vivir en un piso en Ámsterdam, en lugar de jardín no teníamos sino unas cuantas macetas en el balcón. Siempre recordaré, pues, el entusiasmo y orgullo con que mi madre creaba y mantenía esas macetas. ¡Eran el tema de conversación del vecindario!

Debo mi creatividad y pasión por las artes visuales a que mi madre y mi padre las alimentaran. Mi madre estaba involucrada en la industria de la alta costura y mi padre, en el mundo de los automóviles clásicos, ambas empresas decisivamente visuales. Ellos siempre me apoyaron cuando "jugaba con flores" dejándome tomar mi primer curso de arreglos florales con mi (futuro) mentor, Abel Verheijen.

Agradezco el haber estudiado con Abel bajo el antiguo régimen de aprendizaje europeo, prácticamente, desaparecido. Él me tomó, bajo su tutela, a los trece, y me mostró el mundo floral de los maestros diseñadores holandeses, al tiempo en que

Dutch master designers as we traveled to exhibitions and events throughout Europe. Abel is one of a kind. I owe him more than I can ever express.

My parents also supported my decision to go to London for a year at age 19, after which I departed for America as an exchange student. My first year in California was at the invitation of Bill and Anita Buerger, who at the time were cymbidium and strelitzia growers in Encinitas. They, as my American parents, supported and guided me in whatever I dreamt of

doing. Now, 27 years later, as a Dutch American, I have Bill and Anita to thank for my good fortune in the United States.

My first experience with retail design in the U.S. was at the invitation of Dean White and the late Joyce White AIFD. Dean and Joyce took me into their home and exposed me to the American way of "doing flowers," interiors, and showmanship! I will always be grateful for their guidance.

viajábamos a exhibiciones y eventos, por toda Europa. Abel es único. Le debo mucho más de lo que pueda llegar a expresar.

Mis padres también apoyaron mi decisión de ir un año a Londres, a los 19, para de ahí partir a América, en intercambio estudiantil. Mi primer año en California fue a invitación de Bill y Anita Buerger, quienes en aquel tiempo cultivaban orquídeas (cymbidium) y aves del paraíso (sterilitzia), en Encinitas. Ellos, mis padres estadounidenses, me apoyaron y guiaron en todo cuanto soñé realizar. Ahora, 27 años

después, como holandés-americano, agradezco a Bill y a Anita mi buena fortuna en Estados Unidos.

Mi primera experiencia en diseño comercial en este país fue a la invitación de Dean y la ya desaparecida Joyce White (miembro del Instituto Americano de Diseñadores de Flores-AIFD). Dean y Joyce me abrieron su casa, mostrándome el estilo americano del "arreglo floral", para interiores y exposición. Siempre agradeceré su guía.

NATURE'S ART
EL ARTE DE LA NATURALEZA

Why do you hold this book in your hand? Because you feel a fundamental human attraction to the meaningful beauty of flowers.

The need goes further than wanting to enjoy flowers in nature, in fields and forests and gardens. We feel the impulse to bring flowers indoors, to present them as gifts, in a way that harmonizes nature and culture. The craft of bouquet making is as ancient as this impulse, and as universal. Anyone can learn the basic techniques, which also provide the foundation for a sophisticated, evolving art form.

The medium of the art form is botanical material—which is why, to attain the heights of floral design, it's important also to study botany and horticulture, as students of professional floristry do in my home country, the Netherlands. In nature as in

¿Por qué tiene ahora este libro en sus manos? Tal vez por atracción, fundamentalmente humana, hacia la significativa belleza de las flores.

Esa necesidad supera el querer disfrutar de las flores en la naturaleza, en campos, bosques y jardines. Sentimos el impulso de llevarlas a casa, de darlas de regalo, buscando armonizar naturaleza y cultura. El oficio de hacer arreglos es tan antiguo como este impulso, tan universal. Cualquiera aprende técnicas básicas, fundamento de una forma de arte sofisticada, en evolución.

El medio de este arte es el material botánico—de ahí que para llegar alto en diseño floral sea importante aprender botánica y horticultura, como quienes se forman en floristería profesional, en mi país natal, Holanda. En la naturaleza, en el mejor de los diseños, la forma deriva de la función. Entender a las plantas—cómo crecen y por qué sus hermosas

the best of modern design, form follows function. Understanding plants—how they grow and why their beautiful forms represent an evolutionary adaptation—contributes to a sense of what works in floral design, what goes together and why. It opens your eyes to nature's subtle colors and exquisite detail.

formas trazan su adaptación evolutiva—da sentido a lo que funciona en un diseño floral; lo que va junto y por qué. Abre sus ojos a los colores sutiles y a los detalles exquisitos de la naturaleza.

Which brings us back to why we give flowers and place them in our homes. Making bouquets is a way of understanding and appreciating nature, blending it into our lives. If this book helps you to do that, it will have served its purpose.

Lo anterior lleva a entender por regalamos o damos a las flores un lugar en casa. El confeccionar ramos ayuda a entender y apreciar a la naturaleza, mezclándola con nuestras vidas. Si este libro lo ayuda a realizar eso, habrá cumplido su propósito.

CONTENTS
CONTENIDO

VAMOS A COMENZAR

GETTING STARTED

THE HAND-TIED BOUQUET: HISTORY AND CULTURE

EL RAMO DE MANO: HISTORIA Y CULTURA

The hand-tied bouquet has a long tradition in European fashion and style. From the late Middle Ages, ladies—and gentlemen—of rank and wealth carried "nosegays" in the hand, defined as a "fragrant cluster of flowers . . . originally used to mask unpleasant odors" in the *Book of Floral Terminology* published by the American Institute of Floral Designers (AIFD). In nineteenth-century England, these nosegays, known as tussie-mussies, were first tied in the hand, then placed in ornate holders specially designed for the purpose. Gentlemen and ladies exchanged tussie-mussies as romantic gifts, choosing the selection of flowers carefully according to the published dictionary that translated "the language of flowers."

As home décor, hand-tied bouquets have reflected the stylistic sensibility of the period—for example, mid-nineteenth-century Germany, when the Biedermeier bouquet, often made with concentric circles of flowers and always in a perfect dome, expressed the aspirations and orderly aesthetic of the emerging middle class.

Today's hand-tied bouquets can draw on the vocabulary of this wide-ranging tradition to articulate modern emotions and ideas about how to live at home, with flowers.

Confeccionar ramos de mano es tradición antigua en la moda y el estilo europeos. Desde finales de la Edad Media, damas—y caballeros—de rango y riqueza portaban "ramilletes" de mano, definidos en el libro de terminología floral, del Instituto Americano de Diseñadores de Flores (AIFD), *como " fragante conjunto de flores . . . originalmente utilizado para ocultar olores desagradables." En la Inglaterra del siglo diecinueve, esos ramilletes, conocidos como* ramitos victorianos, *se llevaban en la muñeca para luego ponerse en vasijas de ornato, diseñadas con ese fin. Damas y caballeros intercambiaban ramitos de obsequio romántico, eligiendo con cuidado sus flores, en base al diccionario que traducía "el lenguaje de las plantas".*

Los ramos, decoración casera, reflejaban la sensibilidad estilística del período. Así Alemania a mediados del siglo diecinueve, por ejemplo, donde el ramo Biedermeier, a menudo hecho de círculos concéntricos de flores en perfecto domo, expresaba las aspiraciones y el orden estético de la emergente clase media.

Hoy, los ramos de mano toman el vocabulario de esta lejana tradición, articulando emociones e ideas modernas al modo como se vive en casa, con flores.

CHOOSING FLOWERS
ELEGIR LAS FLORES

In selecting flowers for a bouquet, most people are quick to look at **color**. Depending on their mood, intuition, and the colors that predominate in their homes, they may lean toward brights or pastels, a monochromatic (all one color) or analogous color scheme (closely related colors, such as yellow and orange, orange and red, or red and burgundy). We'll show more about the use of color throughout this book.

*La mayoría se fija rápidamente en el **color** al elegir las flores de un ramo. Dependiendo de estado de ánimo, intuición o los colores predominantes del hogar, uno se inclina por colores brillantes o tonos pastel; esquemas monocromáticos (un solo color) o análogos (colores relacionados entre sí, como amarillo y naranja, naranja y rojo, rojo y borgoña). Le mostraremos más del uso del color a través de este libro.*

Form and **texture** are important elements as well. Texture relates to color, and you'll see many examples of this principle in the bouquets. In choosing flower forms, it's useful to think of them in four basic types: mass, line, filler, and form flowers (illustrated on the following pages). Different combinations of these flowers create different effects.

Forma y textura son elementos igualmente importantes. Textura y color se relacionan. Verá muchos ejemplos de este principio en los arreglos. Al escoger la forma de las flores, sirve pensar en ellas en cuatro tipos básicos: Volumen, líneas, relleno o formas (ilustradas en las siguientes páginas). Las diversas combinaciones de estas flores producen efectos distintos.

MASS

Mass flowers act on the eye like points or circles: they provide a resting place, add volume to the design, and combine easily to make a smooth surface. Identification of the flowers in this photo appears on page 130.

Flores de volumen actúan sobre el ojo como puntos o círculos: proporcionan un descanso, agregan sustancia al diseño y se combinan, fácilmente, para crear superficies lisas. La identificación de las flores en esta foto aparece en la página 130.

Line flowers break up the surface of a bouquet. Depending on how the bouquet is made, they emphasize its radial or parallel structure. Because they emerge from the bouquet into the space around it, not closely packed, they make for an airy feeling. Identification of the flowers in this photo appears on page 131.

Flores lineales rompen la superficie del arreglo. Dependiendo de cómo éste se confeccione, las líneas enfatizan su estructura radial o paralela. Estas flores producen una sensación aérea, pues sobresalen del resto del ramo, fuertemente unido, hacia el espacio circundante. La identificación de las flores en esta foto aparece en la página 131.

Filler flowers fill in empty spaces, complement the color scheme, and add frilly or delicate textures to the mix. Identification of the flowers in this photo appears on page 132.

Flores de relleno sirven para ocupar espacios vacíos, completar un patrón de color y agregar sus texturas silvestres o delicadas al conjunto. La identificación de las flores en esta foto aparece en la página 132.

FORM

Form flowers impose their distinctive shapes on the eye. Like line flowers, they require space around the flower to be fully appreciated. Identification of the flowers in this photo appears on page 133.

Flores de forma imponen al ojo sus figuras distintivas. Como las líneas, requieren de espacio alrededor de sí para ser debidamente apreciadas. La identificación de las flores en esta foto aparece en la página 133.

TWIGS
BERRIES
BUDS
PODS

As with colors and forms, textures can be combined to create either unity or contrast. Either can be pleasing. If your materials are all of the same hue, you may choose to vary the texture, and the contrast between matte and shiny, soft and firm, rough and delicate textures will be all the more evident. Don't neglect non-flower botanical materials—**twigs, berries, buds** and **pods**—that offer diverse textures and a range of stylistic moods. Identification of the plant materials in this photo appears on page 134.

*Al igual que con colores y formas, las texturas se combinan para crear unidad o contraste, ambos igualmente placenteros. Cuando los materiales son del mismo tono se puede variar texturas; el contraste entre mate y brillante, suave y firme, áspero y delicado será evidente. No descuide los materiales botánicos no florales—**ramas, bayas, botones y vainas**—que brindan una gama de texturas y variaciones estilísticas. La identificación de los materiales de planta en esta foto aparece en la página 134.*

Yellow green is seen in young leaves and in plants that grow in intense light, such as tropical plants. It combines well with flowers in warm hues.

El verde amarillento puede verse en hojas jóvenes y en plantas que crecen bajo la luz intensa, como las tropicales. Combina bien con flores de tonos cálidos.

Gray green and silvery tones are often found in plants that grow in a dry landscape. They're especially apt for bouquets placed in silver containers.

Los verdes grisáceos y los tonos plateados son a menudo hallados en las plantas que crecen en paisajes secos. Van bien con ramos que serán colocados en bases de plata.

Blue green foliage grows in shade and includes most dark, deep greens. It complements cool color schemes.

El azul verde crece bajo la sombra e incluye la mayor parte de verdes oscuros o profundos. Es un buen complemento de los colores fríos.

Bronze, burgundy, and other reddish-toned foliage is widespread in nature, an effective way to underscore the many reds in the flower kingdom.

Los bronces, borgoña y otros tonos rojizos se dan en follajes bastante comunes, lo que lleva a muchos a subestimar su presencia abundante en el reino de las flores.

Other variegated colors and patterns are common in tropical plants from crotons to cordyline. They add spice to a tropical or any vividly colored bouquet.

Otros colores y patrones variopintos son comunes en plantas tropicales, desde las cascarillas (croton eluteria) hasta las cordilíneas (cordyline terminalis). Estos agregan vivacidad a los ramos tropicales o a los de colores encendidos.

CHOOSING FOLIAGE
ESCOGER FOLLAJE

Since foliage is usually attached to the flower stem, it is often automatically a part of the design. Most foliage is green, simply because all photosynthetic plants rely on chlorophyll for energy. Many floral designers consider green a "neutral" color, so universal that it can be discounted in planning a color scheme for a bouquet. There are different tints, tones, and shades of green, however, as well as other colors of foliage. Matching the foliage to the predominant colors in your bouquet has a subtle but powerful impact.

El follaje va adherido al tallo de la flor y es automáticamente parte de su diseño. En su mayoría es verde, dado que todas las plantas fotosintéticas dependen de la clorofila como fuente de energía. Muchos diseñadores florales consideran al verde color "neutral", tan universal que, al planear el esquema de un ramo, éste no cuente como tal. Hay distintos matices, tintes y tonos de verde, también distintos colores de follaje. El combinar el follaje con los colores predominantes de un ramo produce un impacto sutil pero poderoso.

THE RIGHT VESSEL
EL RECIPIENTE ADECUADO

When it's time to place your bouquet in a vase, select one that works both aesthetically and practically. Aside from its color (unless it's clear glass) and finish, it should be sturdy and of a weight and size appropriate to the size of your bouquet.

Some container materials are better than others. Metal can interact with the acidifiers in flower food, releasing metallic ions into the water that are not good for the flowers. If you want to use a

Cuando llega el momento de colocar el ramo en un jarrón, querrá elegir uno que sea a la vez funcional y estético. Además del color (salvo que sea transparente) y el acabado, deberá ser resistente, y de peso y tamaño aproximados al tamaño del ramo.

__Algunos contenedores son mejores que otros.__ El metal puede actuar sobre los acidificantes del alimento, liberando iones metálicos que flotan en el agua y pueden perjudicar a

metal vase, place a glass or plastic one inside it. Plastic and crystal are good choices, but over time both can develop small pitted areas where bacteria can settle that are difficult to clean thoroughly. The ideal choice is glass or glazed ceramic.

las flores. Al usar un florero de metal, coloque en su interior otro de vidrio o plástico. Plástico y cristal son buenas elecciones pero, a través del tiempo, en ambos pueden aparecer pequeñas hendiduras que alojan bacterias difíciles de eliminar con la limpieza. Alternativas ideales son el vidrio o la cerámica vidriada.

Pay special attention to the size of the opening and water reservoir. A large opening accommodates a large bouquet but won't support the stems, if it's too wide, as well as a smaller one. If the vase is one you would use to hold a medium-sized bouquet, it should hold at least a quart, or liter, of water (mixed with flower food)—enough to last about a week.

Ponga especial atención al tamaño y apertura de su recipiente. *Una apertura ancha permite acomodar ramos grandes, pero no ofrece a los tallos el soporte adecuado, si es demasiado ancha; tampoco si es demasiado angosta. Un jarrón que usaría para un ramo de tamaño mediano, deberá contener un cuarto, un litro, de agua (mezclado con alimento para flores)—el suficiente para durar una semana.*

MAKING FLOWERS LAST
COMO LOGRAR QUE LOS FLORES DUREN

Cut flowers are alive. Though cut off from their roots, they continue their natural processes of blooming and maturing, eventually fading and dying—at a faster or slower rate, depending on the care you give them. They need not only water but also nutrients (glucose), which they absorb from the bottom of the stem, bringing the nutrient solution up through the stem by means of a vascular system (the xylem vessels). When flowers die too soon, it's usually because the lowest cells in the vascular system have become clogged with micro-organisms, organic matter, and air bubbles. The temperature of the flowers and the water also influences their metabolism: coolness slows it down, warmth speeds it up. This is why, if you want flowers to last longer, it helps to place them in a cool spot. After you've selected the right flowers and the right vase, take the right steps to keep them looking fresh as long as possible.

Las flores cortadas están vivas. A pesar de haber sido separadas de sus raíces, éstas continúan su proceso natural de florecimiento y madurez, hasta marchitarse y morir—tan rápido o tan lento como sus tiernos cuidados lo permitan. No sólo necesitan agua sino también nutrientes (glucosa), mismos que absorben desde la punta del tallo, para transportarlos hacia la flor con la ayuda de un sistema vascular (xylem). Cuando las flores mueren demasiado pronto se debe a que las células inferiores del tejido vascular son obstruidas por micro-organismos, materia orgánica y burbujas. La temperatura de las flores y el agua también influye sobre su metabolismo: el frío lo disminuye y el calor lo acelera. De ahí que si quiere que sus flores duren más tiempo, le ayudará mantenerlas en un sitio fresco. Una vez que haya seleccionado las flores y el florero adecuados, deberá dar los pasos correctos para mantener frescas sus flores, el mayor tiempo posible.

Use a clean vase. Scrub vases with soap and a brush directly after use. Use bleach or a disinfecting vase cleaner.

Use a cut-flower-food solution. In addition to nutrients, Chrysal cut-flower food contains an antimicrobial agent and an acidifier to lower the pH. It's important for these elements to be in balance with each other and in correct proportion to the water.

Lacking the scientific formulation of commercial flower food, home remedies, such as sugar water, aspirin, or soft drinks do more harm than good. When using cut-flower food, be sure to mix it according to directions, measuring carefully. There are also specialty flower foods fine-tuned to the physiological needs of different types of flowers, such as woody-stemmed flowers, lilies, and bulb flowers.

Utilice un jarrón limpio. Talle sus jarrones con jabón y cepillo justo después de usarlos. Use cloro o desinfectante para floreros.

Utilice alimento especial para flores cortadas.
Además de nutrientes, Chrysal para flores cortadas contiene un agente antibacterial y un acidificador que disminuye el pH. Es importante que estos elementos se equilibren uno

a otro, en proporción correcta con el agua. Al no tener la fórmula científica del alimento comercial para flores, los remedios caseros como agua azucarada, aspirina o refrescos dañan más de lo que ayudan. Mida el alimento con cuidado y siga las instrucciones al mezclarlo. Hay alimento especial para flores, acorde a las necesidades fisiológicas de los distintos tipos, ya sean flores de tallo de madera, lilas o bulbos.

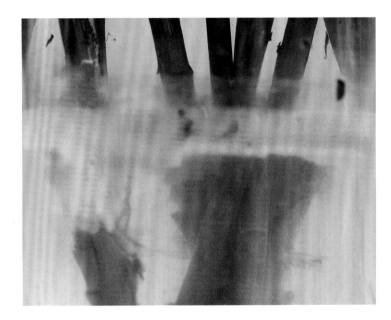

Scum lines in the vase result when micro-organisms settle on the inside, the water level drops and the settled scum dries out. You should never let vases get this dirty, but if they do, they should be cleaned with firm brushing and soaking using a soft, non-aggressive cleaning agent or vase cleaning tablets.

La película que se forma sobre el florero se debe a micro-organismos que se alojan en su interior. Cuando el nivel del agua baja, la capa depositada se seca. Nunca debe dejar sus floreros ensuciarse así. Cuando esto ocurra debe limpiarlos cepillando firmemente y usando abundante detergente suave, no agresivo, o las tabletas especiales para floreros.

Flowers "breathe," releasing moisture to the air continually. It's been said that the life of a cut flower is a race between water loss and water intake. A clear flower food, which comes in both a powdered and a liquid form, discourages the growth of micro-organisms, keeping the water clean and the stem ends clear so they can absorb both water and nutrients.

Las flores "respiran" liberando humedad en el aire, continuamente. Ha sido dicho que la vida de una flor cortada es una carrera entre la pérdida de agua y su ingestión. Un alimento transparente, de polvo o líquido, previene el crecimiento de micro organismos, manteniendo el agua limpia y las puntas de los tallos libres para poder absorber el agua y los nutrientes.

Use clean, room-temperature water to make the solution. Cold water is OK too. Warm water is not as good, since it is more likely to contain microorganisms and air bubbles that can clog the stems. Cut-flower food does not require warm water to dissolve completely.

Utilice agua limpia, a temperatura ambiente, al preparar la solución. El agua fría también sirve. El agua tibia no es tan buena, ya que es factible que contenga microorganismos y burbujas que pudieran obstruir los tallos. El alimento para flores cortadas no requiere de agua tibia para disolverse bien.

Remove foliage that will be below the water line. Submerged leaves may contribute to the growth of bacteria in the water. Be careful, however, not to damage the stem "bark" or skin. The xylem vessels that carry nutrient-bearing flower-food solution from the bottom of the stem to the flowers lie close to the outside of the stem and can be easily damaged with careless use of a knife. Equipment designed to remove leaves and thorns "efficiently" is even more likely to cause such damage.

Elimine el follaje que pueda quedar bajo el agua. Las hojas sumergidas contribuyen al crecimiento de bacterias flotantes. Tenga cuidado de no dañar "la corteza" o piel del tallo. El tejido vascular, transmisor de la solución que contiene los nutrientes, del tallo hacia la flor, se queda cerca del exterior del tallo y puede ser dañado fácilmente mediante el uso descuidado de un cuchillo. El equipo diseñado para remover hojas y espinas "eficientemente" puede dañar aún más.

A magnified cross-section of a flower stem reveals the ring of spongy-looking xylem vessels close to the outside of the stem. These are the cells responsible for transporting water and dissolved nutrients up the stem to the flower. When they become blocked with micro-organisms or debris, the flower can no longer "drink." The right photo shows blocked xylem vessels in a longitudinal cut.

Al hacer un corte en el tallo y magnificarlo con una lupa, se revela un círculo de tejido esponjoso, flotando cerca del exterior del tallo. Se trata de vasos responsables de transportar el agua y los nutrientes, disueltos en ella, del tallo hacia la flor. Cuando el tallo es obstruido por microorganismos o por partículas de desecho, la flor deja de "beber". Una foto del corte longitudinal muestra ese tejido atrapado.

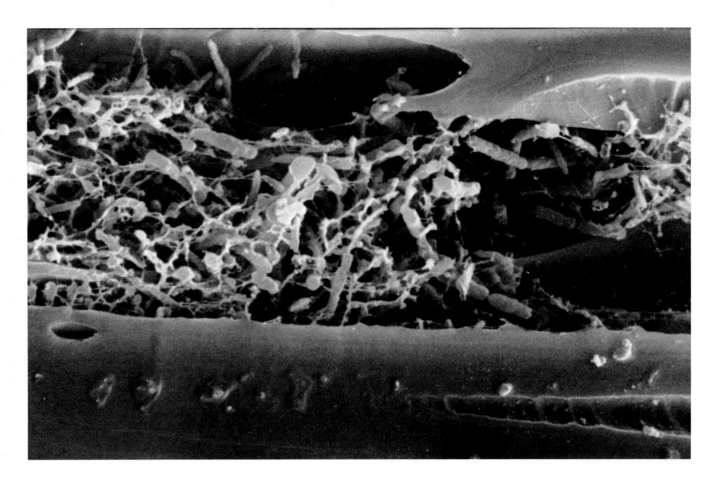

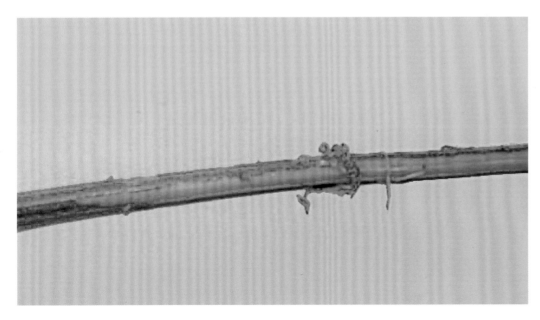

THE WRONG WAY: In preparing flowers for the vase, it's important to remove any leaves that would otherwise be submerged in a solution of water and flower food—but do it carefully, with a sharp knife. Organic matter from the damaged stem, released into the water, encourages the growth of micro-organisms. Never scrape the stem.

LA MANERA INCORRECTA: Al preparar las flores para la base de su arreglo es importante remover cualquier hoja que pudiera quedar sumergida en la solución de agua y alimento para flores—hágalo con cuidado con un cuchillo filoso. Materia orgánica procedente del tallo flotará en el agua, activando el crecimiento de micro-organismos. Nunca raspe el tallo.

Re-cut the stems. Using a clean, sharp knife, remove one to two inches from the base of the stem. The idea is to cut away the part of the stem that has become dried out, if the flower has been out of water, or blocked with micro-organisms and air bubbles, if the flower has been in water that was allowed to become clouded with debris and microbial growth. Professionals slice the stems at a 45-degree angle. Too sharp an angle can also damage the cells and lead to blockage. Some professionals use an underwater cutter to re-cut the stems. However, it's not necessary to cut the stems underwater if you use a cut flower food, which contains ingredients to clear the way for water uptake.

If you need to top up the vase, use more water with flower food. Properly mixed flower food will keep the water clear and clean over the life of the bouquet.

Recortar los tallos. Remueva una o dos pulgadas de la punta del tallo con un cuchillo filoso y limpio. La idea es cortar lo seco, cuando la flor ha estado fuera del agua o el tallo ha sido bloqueado por micro-organismos y burbujas si el agua se dejó enturbiar. Los profesionales cortan los tallos en un ángulo de 45 grados. Un ángulo muy pronunciado puede dañar las células y dejar que se tapen. Algunos utilizan un instrumento sumergible para recortar los tallos. No es necesario cortarlos bajo el agua si utiliza comida especial que contenga ingredientes que ayuden a liberar las vías y permitan a la flor beber.

Si necesita llenar el florero, utilice más agua que nutriente. El alimento para flores, mezclado correctamente, mantendrá el agua transparente y limpia durante la vida de su ramo.

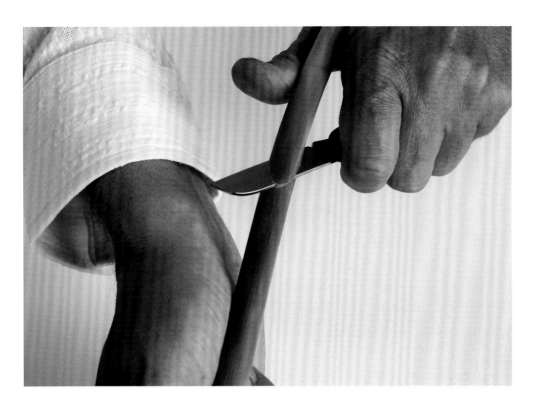

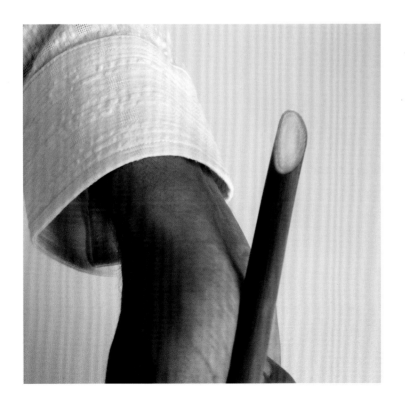

A sharp, clean knife is the best cutting tool, although sharp pruning shears provide a second-best alternative. A 45-degree angle gives the cleanest cut, with the least stem damage. Re-cutting stem ends removes cells that have become blocked with micro-organisms, air bubbles or debris.

The angle of the cut is especially important when stems will be inserted into floral foam, as you may wish to do in creating a "faux hand-tied bouquet" (see the section "More than Meets the Eye" in this book.) Like the flower stem itself, floral foam has a cellular structure. When the two are cleanly connected, the foam becomes an extension of the stem, providing water and nutrients. A flat-cut stem, however, crushes the foam, damaging its cellular structure. An angle-cut stem slides easily into the foam, which then grips it, holding the stem in place. All flowers, but especially roses, benefit from an angle cut when placed in foam.

Un cuchillo filoso y limpio es el mejor instrumento para cortar, aunque las tijeras podadoras bien afiladas sean la siguiente opción. El corte más preciso y menos dañino para el tallo se hace en ángulo de 45 grados. Recortar las puntas de los tallos elimina células bloqueadas por micro-organismos, burbujas o desecho.

El ángulo del corte es especialmente importante cuando se inserta a los tallos en espuma floral, como hará cuando fabrique un "falso ramo de mano" (ver sección "More than Meets the Eye" en este libro). Al igual que el propio tallo, la espuma floral tiene una estructura celular que actúa como si fuese su extensión, proveyendo agua y nutrientes, cuando ambos están limpiamente conectados. Un corte plano, destruye la espuma, dañando esa estructura. El tallo cortado en ángulo se desliza fácilmente en la espuma, que lo agarra con firmeza. Todas las flores, especialmente las rosas, se benefician del corte en ángulo al ser colocadas en la espuma.

THE RIGHT MIX
LA MEZCLA ADECUADA

Whether on the plant or cut, some flowers naturally have a longer life than others. In selecting flowers for a bouquet, you want to combine those with a similar vase life and not, for example, pair short-lived sweet-peas with long-lived cymbidium orchids.

The vase life of cut flowers also depends on their maturity. A rosebud has a longer vase life ahead of it than a fully open rose. Your choice of one or the other depends on the flower, the season, and the purpose for which you are making the bouquet: is it for a party tonight, or for a place in the home where it should last at least a week?

Ya sea en la planta o cortadas, algunas flores duran, natu-ralmente, más que otras. Al seleccionar las flores para un ramo, querrá combinar aquellas que tengan extensión de vida similar en el jarrón y no, por ejemplo, chícharos efímeros con orquídeas cymbidium de larga vida.

La vida de las flores en un jarrón depende también de su madurez. Un botón de rosa vivirá más, en un florero, que una rosa ya abierta. Su elección de una u otra depende de la flor, la estación, el propósito para el que usted hace su ramo: ¿lo utilizará en una fiesta en la noche, o lo colocará en la casa, adonde deberá durar, por lo menos, una semana?

LOS RAMOS

THE BOUQUETS

TECHNIQUES FOR MAKING HAND-TIED BOUQUETS
TÉCNICAS PARA HACER RAMOS DE MANO

The spiral bouquet is the classic and most widely used of the four methods in the European tradition. For technique, see pages 44–47.

A parallel bouquet is similar, except that the stems are kept parallel. The technique is generally used for flowers with thick, straight stems.

Lacing may be done "in the hand" or by placing the stems directly into the vase. It relies on starting with branched material, or sturdy stems crossing each other, that can lend support to other stems as they are added to the bouquet.

An armature bouquet makes use of a sturdy structure made from branches or vines. Stems are inserted through the structure, which supports them. The technique enables a wide range of forms, from fan- to disk-shaped.

El ramo en espiral es el clásico y más ampliamente usado de cuatro métodos en la tradición europea. La técnica en las páginas 44–47

El ramo paralelo es similar, excepto que sus tallos se mantienen paralelos. Esta técnica es generalmente utilizada en flores con tallos rectos y gruesos.

El entrelazado puede hacerse "en la mano" o colocando los tallos directamente en una base. Este ramo depende de que se inicie con material que se ramifique o con tallos resistentes que se entrecrucen y que sirvan de soporte para otros tallos que vayan agregándose al ramo.

El ramo armazón se sirve de una estructura resistente lograda con ramas y hojas de parra. Los tallos se agregan por toda la estructura que los sostiene. Esta técnica permite lograr un amplio número de formas, desde un abanico hasta un disco.

HOW TO MAKE
A SPIRAL BOUQUET
CÓMO HACER UN RAMO EN ESPIRAL

Begin by preparing the stems (removing lower foliage) and sorting them into vases. Place the first stem in the palm of one hand, holding it between thumb and forefinger. I'm left-handed, so I hold the stems in my right hand and add them to the growing bundle with my left (**1**). Add several more stems, until you have a still-slender foundation bundle. Then, as the bundle thickens, the spiral begins (**2, 3**).

Add new stems by slipping them under your thumb at an angle almost perpendicular to the bundle, then pulling down to rotate the stem into position (**4, 5**). As you add more stems, turn the entire bouquet in your hand, rotating it clockwise. This allows you to add stems evenly to all sides. Keep your hand open as the bundle grows. Don't make a fist; hold the bundle at the binding point with just your thumb and fore-finger so the stems can fan out above and below (**6**).

Comience preparando los tallos (remueva el follaje inferior) y separándolos en distintos floreros. Coloque el primer tallo en la palma de una mano, sosteniéndolo entre el pulgar y el índice. Soy zurdo, de modo que sostengo los tallos con la mano derecha y los voy agregando al manojo con la izquierda (1). Agregue muchos tallos, hasta que logre un haz delgado y firme. A medida en que éste aumente, la espiral comienza (2, 3).

Agregue nuevos tallos, deslizándolos bajo su pulgar en ángulo casi perpendicular al manojo y, luego, jalando hacia abajo, rote el tallo hasta acomodarlo (4, 5). Mientras añade más tallos, gire el ramo sobre su mano, en dirección de las manecillas del reloj. Podrá ir aumentando tallos, equilibrada-mente, por todos lados. Mantenga su mano abierta a medida que el manojo crece. No forme un puño; sostenga su manojo en el punto de unión con tan solo pulgar e índice dejando que los tallos se abran en abanico arriba y abajo (6).

2

3

5

6

On the outside of the bundle, you may wish to add a leafy collar, still angling the stems (**7, 8**). Tie your bouquet at the binding point (**9**).

*Al exterior del manojo, puede querer agregar un anillo de hojas, los tallos aún en ángulo (**7, 8**). Asegure su ramo en el punto de unión (**9**).*

8

9

When the bouquet is tied off, re-cut the bottoms of the stems so they are all the same length, using sharp pruning shears. Voilà! Your bouquet is complete. If it is well constructed, with an even distribution of materials, and the stems properly trimmed, the bouquet will stand up by itself on a flat surface. The spiral structure allows the flower heads to fan out into a dome, which may be smooth or frothy—as in this medley of callas, stock, Queen Anne's lace, matricaria, and sycamore leaves.

Cuando asegure su ramo, recorte las puntas de los tallos para que tengan el mismo largo. Utilice tijeras podadoras filosas. ¡Voilà! Su ramo está terminado. Si lo construyó bien, equilibrando sus materiales y recortando adecuadamente sus tallos, su ramo se erguirá por sí mismo en una superficie plana. La estructura espiral permite a las cabezas de las flores distribuirse en abanico hasta formar un domo, que puede ser liso o irregular—como en esta mezcla lilas calla, flor de zanahoria, matricaria y hojas de sicomoro.

Country Frills Dinámica campestre

Two typical features of spiral technique are easily seen in this miniature bouquet featuring grape hyacinths: the stems form a pleasing, swirling pattern, and the surface of the bouquet is rounded and compact. When all the stems have been assembled in the hand, the bouquet is bound with twine, which can then be covered with decorative ribbon. Here the blue of the grape hyacinths is complemented by silvery dusty miller and gray-green eucalyptus foliage, and their beaded texture by seeded eucalyptus. Last to be added to the bouquet was a ring of dusty-miller foliage forming a collar that frames the flowers.

Dos rasgos típicos de la técnica de la espiral se ven fácilmente en este ramo en miniatura caracterizado por los jacintos color uva: los tallos forman un placentero patrón en espiral y la superficie del ramo es redonda y compacta. Cuando todos los tallos se reúnen en la mano, el ramo se ata con ramillas, lo que puede ser cubierto con listón decorativo. Aquí, el azul de los jacintos es complementado con centaurea cenicienta plateada y follaje verde grisáceo de eucalipto; la textura en forma de cuentas es lograda por las vainas del eucalipto. Lo último por agregar al ramo es el anillo de hojas de la centaura que circunda y enmarca las flores.

Harmony at Home   Armonía en el hogar

In the home, the colors and pattern of a spiral bouquet can make a stunning complement to textiles and other decorative accessories. Dahlias, leucospermum (pincushion protea), hypericum berries, and nubbly annual scabiosa mingle orange-reds and bluish reds in an intricate design that sings in harmony with this table runner and ornamental vase. The blue-green of the ceramic pot matches the foliage in the bouquet, a color complement to the reds.

En el hogar, los colores y patrones de un ramo en espiral pueden ser el complemento contundente para los textiles y demás accesorios decorativos. Las dalias, las proteas de acerico, las bayas de hipéricum y las annual scabiosa permiten la mezcla de rojos anaranjados, rojos azulados y todo el intrincado diseño que canta en armonía con este pasillo de mesa y la base ornamental. El azul verde de la maceta de cerámica combina con el follaje del arreglo y ofrece un complemento colorido a los rojos.

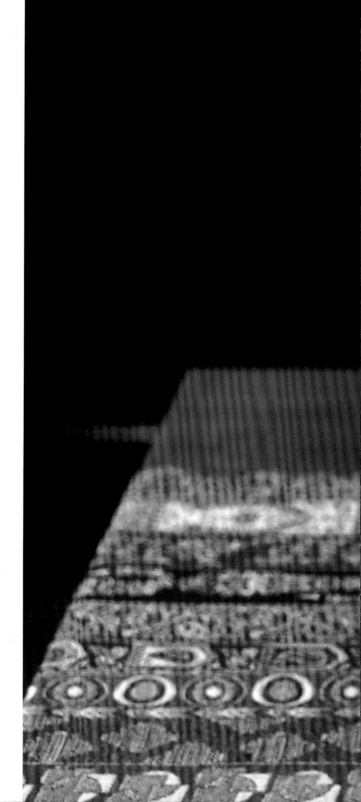

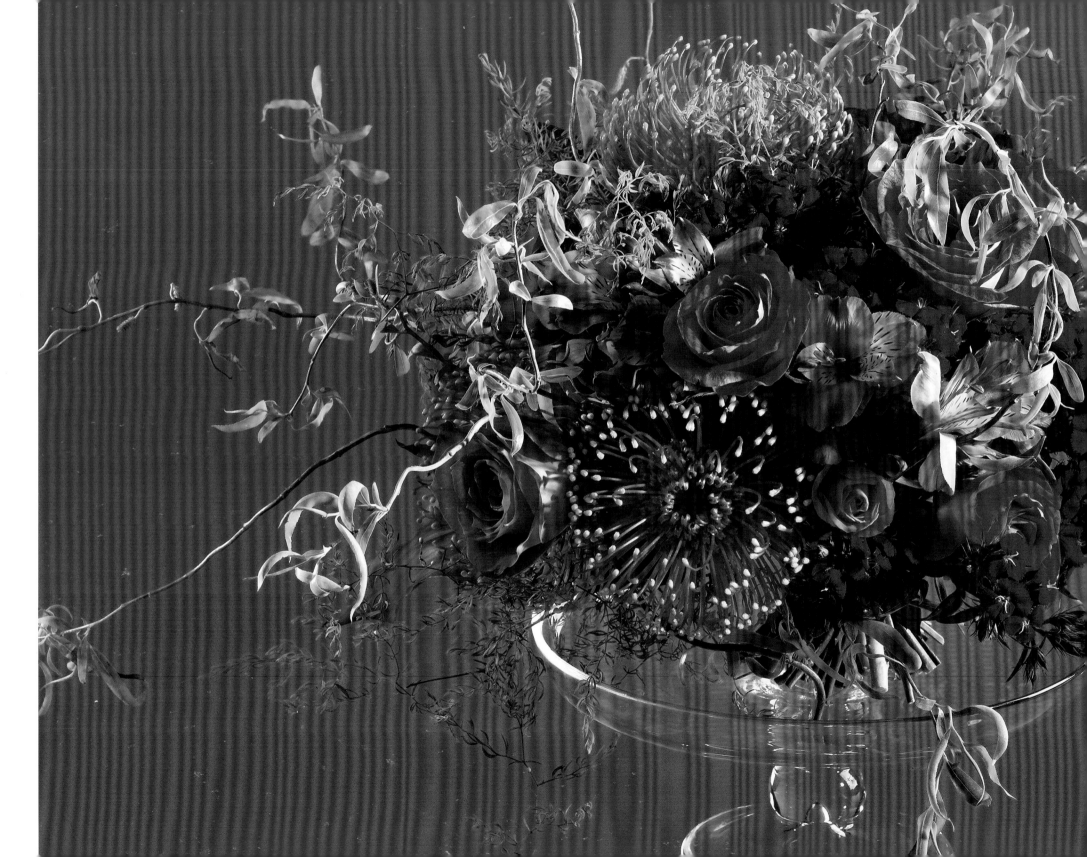

On Point   De puntas

Here's another example of a spiral bouquet assembled in such a way that the surface is less compact, offering more depth to the eye. Some flowers (roses and leucospermum) emerge more prominently than others (alstroemeria and sweet William), and the sinuous tips of curly willow dance over the bouquet, adding a sense of lively motion. Its sturdy, spiral construction permits a stylish option for display, elevated on a clear glass cake plate with a rim high enough to hold water mixed with flower food.

He aquí otro ejemplo de un ramo en espiral unido de tal modo que su superficie es menos compacta, ofreciendo más profundidad al ojo. Algunas flores (rosas y leucospermum) emergen más notoriamente que otras (lilas peregrinas y sweet William). Las puntas sinuosas del sauce abigarrado, se desplazan por este arreglo, añadiendo una sensación de movimiento vivaz. La resistente construcción en espiral permite la opción para mesa de gran estilo, elevada sobre un plato de pastel transparente con un borde lo suficientemente alto para contener la mezcla de alimento para flores.

Red Velvet   Terciopelo rojo

Here's a secret to combining colors: nothing could bring out the deep, velvety red of 'Black Baccara' roses and fuzzy kangaroo paws like the tiny red centers of these euphorbia flowers, whose tender light green stands out against the dark red. The roses and kangaroo paws offer a contrast in form that is all the more evident because they are so similar in color and texture. Birch twigs add yet another harmonious contrast.

He aquí un secreto para combinar colores: nada podría hacer resaltar mejor el rojo profundo y aterciopelado de las rosas (negro Baccara) o de las garigoleadas patas de canguro (anigozanthus) que los pequeños bulbos de la euphorbia, cuyos verdes claros y tiernos hacen contraste con los rojos. Las rosas y las patas de canguro ofrecen un contraste de formas que se hace muy evidente, debido a que ambos son similares en color y textura. Las ramas de abedul contribuyen, aún más, al armonioso contraste.

Spice Mix · Mezcla vivaz

Monochromatic (tints, tones, and shades of the same color) and analogous color schemes (in a narrow range of closely related colors) are among the easiest and most pleasing to assemble. Spray roses, like deep-orange 'Babe', create natural clusters of color that make a stronger impact from the grouping of blossoms. In this bouquet, the pollen on the tulip stamens holds a hint of saffron yellow that is answered in the hue of the orchids, spotted with cinnamon that matches the tulip petals. Green leaves in the center of the bouquet sharpen the burnt-orange tones by contrast. A well-chosen ribbon picks up the tulips' subtle sheen.

Los esquemas monocromáticos (tintes tonos y matices de un solo color) y análogos (en una variedad de colores relacionados entre sí) se cuentan entre las más fáciles y placenteras formas de ensamblaje. Los ramos de rosas en anaranjado profundo, naturalmente agrupados, producen gran impacto, por el conjunto de botones. En este ramo, el polen sobre los estambres de tulipán mantiene y resalta, discretamente, el amarillo azafrán que se resuelve junto con la tonalidad de las orquídeas, salpicadas de canela y naranja contrastante. El listón, elegido adecuadamente, hace notar el brillo sutil de los tulipanes.

Well Rounded Redondeados

The spherical form of a classic Biedermeier bouquet is seconded by choosing round materials, all in shades of deep wine and silver: Chinese spray carnations, spray roses, and rose hips, with a doily-like collar of protea leaves. For presentation or for a bouquet to carry down the aisle, ribbon bows were added to chenille stems underneath the collar. As a bridal bouquet, this would last out of water for some time, both because of its hardy materials and because of its tight form, such that the stems and blooms support each other. As a décor bouquet, the silvery edging of the Chinese spray carnations is perfectly complemented by a silver vase, which also accords with the rich formality of the bouquet.

La forma esférica del ramo Biedermeier clásico se secunda al elegir materiales también redondos, todos en distintos matices de vino profundo y de plateado. Los brotes de clavel chino, de rosa y las rosas salvajes, llevan un collarín de adorno hecho de hojas de protea. Tanto en una presentación como en un ramo de novia, a los tallos de chenille, bajo el collarín, se les agrega listones en forma de moño. Esto permite, si se trata de un ramo de novia, que dure fuera del agua más tiempo. La firmeza de los materiales y la forma en que se les aprieta hacen que tallos y botones se sostengan, unos a otros. Como ramo ornamental, el borde plateado de los brotes de clavel chino se complementa perfectamente con la base plateada, lo que concuerda también con la rica formalidad del arreglo.

Three in One Tres en uno

When the materials that make up a bouquet are
well chosen, they work equally well to make up one
bouquet or three smaller ones. Texture comes to
the fore when the flowers are all of one color, and
these all-blush flowers offer an array of soft and frilly
textures. Broken into a series of three, as on the
preceding pages, they are linked by the grasses that
are allowed to arc gently between them. The baskets,
equipped with liners, pick up the notes of cream and
tan in the rice flower, cuckoo flower, and oats.

Cuando los materiales que forman un ramo son elegidos con
acierto, funcionan lo mismo para uno que para tres similares,
más pequeños. La textura sobresale cuando las flores son todas
de un mismo color, y estas flores, todas en blanco, ofrecen una
gama de texturas suaves y dinámicas. Al dividirse en una serie
de tres, como en las páginas anteriores, los verdes que forman
un arco discreto entre ellas, las ligan entre sí. Las canastas,
forradas, realzan las notas en crema y café claro de las flores
de arroz, de mostaza (cardamine pratensis) y de avena.

Tropical Fanfare Fanfarria tropical

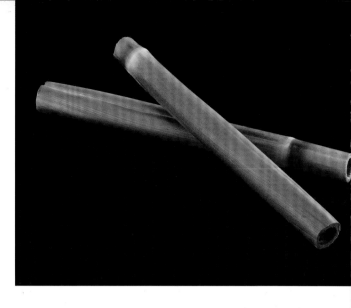

Tropical flowers can be difficult to work with using a spiral technique, because of their heavy stems. One solution is to build the spiral out of sections of green rivercane. The rivercane is hollow, but segmented like bamboo, with partitions inside the stem at the nodes. Each open-ended segment forms a miniature natural water tube. Arrange the sections of rivercane into a spiral. Hold the bundle together with a rubber band, then cover the rubber band with a broad rivercane leaf, held on with double-faced tape. Fill the stems with water mixed with flower food and insert tropical flowers and foliage: here, cymbidium orchids, ginger, bear grass, and variegated cordyline tips, a bundle of grasses attached to one stem.

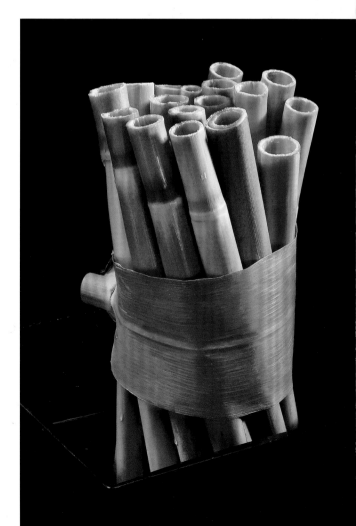

Las flores tropicales dificultan el trabajo cuando se usa la técnica de la espiral. Esto debido a sus pesados tallos. Una solución es seccionar la espiral hecha a base de carrizos. El carrizo es hueco pero segmentado, como el bamboo, con divisiones en los nodos, al interior del tallo. Cada segmento, abierto en sus extremos, forma un tubo de agua natural en miniatura. Acomode los pedazos de carrizo en espiral. Mantenga el conjunto unido utilizando una liga, cubra después la liga con una hoja de junco, ancha, sujetada con un pedazo de cinta adhesiva de doble lado. Llene los tallos de alimento para flores, mezclado con agua, y añada las flores y el follaje tropical: Aquí hay orquídeas, flor de jengibre (zingiberaceae) y hojas de cordilíneas (bromedalias) multiformes, con manojos de pasto, adheridos a cada tallo.

Sheltering Leaves
Hojas protectoras

As you become more adept with spiral technique, you'll want to play with the effects that can be achieved by including materials that extend beyond the traditional smooth, rounded surface. Here, variegated hala leaves were bound into the bouquet, then

Una vez que domine la técnica de la espiral, querrá jugar con los efectos que pueden lograrse al incluir materiales que van más allá de la superficie tradicional, lisa y redonda. Aquí, las hojas multiformes hala (kihalani lauhala) sirven para unir el

bent back in over the top for a sheltering structure that angles in and out among the spikey tips of green dock and over the mix of roses, hydrangea, cockscomb, and ginger.

ramo y luego, dobladas sobre el borde, forman una estructura protectora en ángulo. Hacia afuera van las puntas espinosas de rumex verde y el conjunto de rosas, hortensias, celosía y jengibre.

Sushi Wrap   La envoltura Sushi

One way to make the most of individual flowers is to provide each with its own wrapping. Here, each white gerbera was provided with its own collar of nori, the dried seaweed used in making sushi. The nori is lightweight and its natural dark-green color is reminiscent of leaves. Use double-faced tape to attach the nori to itself and to the flower. Assemble the bouquet using spiral technique, working in branches of huckleberry to diversify the texture, in contrast with the round forms and flat surface of the nori-wrapped gerberas.

Una manera de sacar el mayor provecho de las flores individuales, es dar a cada una su propia envoltura. Aquí, las gerberas blancas llevan un collarín de nori; las algas secas son utilizadas para hacer el sushi. El nori es ligero y su color natural, verde oscuro, evoca el follaje. Utilice cinta adhesiva de doble lado para fijar el nori, tanto a la flor, como a sí mismo. Una su ramo utilizando la técnica de la espiral, incorporando los bulbos de parvifolium para diversificar su textura, en contraste con las formas redondas y las superficies planas de las gerberas envueltas en nori.

Twigs Inside and Out Ramas, adentro y afuera

Twigs add a woodsy, natural texture to bouquets. A vase treatment with twigs complements their inclusion inside the bouquet and ties the look of the bouquet and vase together. Secure the twigs to the outside of a clear glass vase with barked wire, wrapping the wire around the twigs and twisting it onto itself. A flared rim fans the twigs just so. In the completed bouquet, dark twigs swelling with leafbuds stand out against the pale background surface of the white and green flowers: anemones, 'Green Mist' Queen Anne's lace, and waxflower, underscored by scented geranium leaves.

Las ramas añaden el efecto natural de la madera a los ramos. Sobre el florero, un arreglo de ramas remata la apariencia y unidad del ramo y del florero. Asegure las ramas al exterior del florero, transparente, con alambre tejido alrededor de las ramas y torcido sobre sí mismo. La apertura del borde, más ancha, da forma de abanico a las ramas. Una vez terminado el arreglo, ramas oscuras, envolviendo a los brotes, realzan la superficie pálida lograda por las flores blancas y verdes: anémonas, flor de zanahoria y australianas silvestres, subrayadas por las olorosas hojas de geranio.

Tone on Tone Tono sobre tono

Ribbon is a traditional accessory for binding a hand-tied bouquet, but there's no reason why it can't also be incorporated into the bouquet itself—especially when its color and sheen perfectly match some of the flowers, as these twists of moiré ribbon do the lilac tulips and sweet William. The color scheme is brightened with fuchsia roses, alstroemeria, and hot pink boronia. The loops of knotted ribbon are attached to wire "stems" that are added to the bouquet like any other "flower." A vase treatment with ribbon reinforces both the color and the formal, geometric style of the Biedermeier bouquet. A ti leaf is wrapped around the clear glass vase and held on with a rubber band, which is covered with bands of ribbon knotted to echo the bouquet.

El listón es un accesorio tradicional utilizado para unir ramos de mano. Sin embargo, no hay razón por la cual no deba ser incorporado al ramo mismo—especialmente cuando su color y brillo combinen, perfectamente, con algunas flores, como estas ramas de listón de muaré que combinan con los tulipanes lilas y los sweet William. El patrón de color es avivado con las rosas fucsia, alstroemeria, y boronia rosa encendido. Los nudos formados por el listón se fijan a tallos de alambre que se agregan al ramo como cualquier otra "flor". Un jarrón adornado con listón refuerza tanto el color como el estilo de formas geométricas del estilo Biedermeier. Una hoja Ti da la vuelta sobre el florero de vidrio transparente, mantenida con una liga y cubierta, ésta, con tiras de listón anudadas imitando los adornos del ramo.

On the Side   Al lado

Long, straight stems like those of iris can be used
in a spiral bouquet, but they also make an elegant
sheaf when combined in parallel fashion. Leaning
on the rim of a low glass cube, this iris bundle cuts a
dramatic, dynamic diagonal line. Cape honeysuckle
vine wrapped around the bundle lends interest and
organic texture. With all but the smallest leaves
removed, the vine will last as long as the iris.

*Tallos largos y rectos como los de iris pueden ser utilizados
en un ramo en espiral, pero también sirven para formar un
haz elegante cuando éste se confecciona en forma paralela.
Apoyado en el borde de un recipiente bajo de vidrio, en forma
de cubo, el conjunto de iris traza una línea diagonal, dinámi-
ca y dramática. La hoja de madreselva, alrededor del manojo,
aporta una estructura orgánica interesante. Una vez que se
elimina todo, salvo las hojas más pequeñas, la mata durará
tanto tiempo como el iris.*

Inside Out

De adentro hacia afuera

The effect of parallel stems can be achieved with a vase treatment, while the bouquet inside the vase is constructed using spiral technique to obtain a rounded shape. These sunflowers, combined with Chinese elm foliage, emerge from a cylinder covered with segments of sunflower stems. The stem segments are held onto the cylinder by a rubber band that is covered with twine, adding to the illusion of a parallel hand-tied bouquet.

El efecto de los tallos paralelos se logra al trabajar el jarrón, mientras que el ramo, al interior del mismo, es confeccionado mediante la técnica de la espiral que nos da una forma redonda. Estos girasoles, combinados con follaje de olmo chino, emergen de un cilindro cubierto con segmentos de tallos de girasol. Los segmentos de tallo se adhieren al cilindro con la ayuda de una liga que se cubre con ramas, agregando la ilusión de un ramo paralelo, hecho a mano.

Straight Up
Recto

For vases with small openings and slender necks, straight-up-and-down stems work better than spiral bouquets. These small parallel bundles were first assembled and tied in the hand, including their galax-leaf collars, then placed in the vase. The rich hue of the ranunculus and the glazed vases calls out the touches of burgundy in the orchids and galax leaves.

Para jarrones con pequeñas aperturas o cuellos angostos, los tallos rectos, de arriba a abajo, funcionan mejor que los ramos en espiral. Estos conjuntos paralelos pequeños deben unirse y asegurarse en la mano, incluyendo sus collares de hojas de limón, para luego colocarlos en el jarrón. La rica tonalidad del ranunculus y de los jarrones de cerámica vidriada subraya los toques borgoña de las orquídeas y las hojas del limón (galax urceolata).

Branching Out
Ramas hacia afuera

"Lacing" is a technique that's particularly useful with branching material, like the red-leaved photinia included in this bouquet. It can be used in the hand or in the vase. If the twigs or branching stems fork below the center, or binding point, of a hand-tied bouquet, it's difficult to combine them with other stems using spiral technique. Placed in the vase, however, they create a framework to support stems, like the sunflowers and asclepias seen here.

El encaje o entrelazado, es una técnica particularmente útil cuando se cuenta con ramas, como photinia de hojas rojas, entre los materiales del ramo. También puede usarse en la mano o en un jarrón. Si las ramas o tallos se bifurcan más abajo del centro, o del punto de encuentro de un ramo de mano, es difícil combinarlos con otros tallos utilizando la técnica de la espiral. Al ser colocados en un jarrón, las bifurcaciones crean un marco de soporte para los otros tallos, como ocurre con girasoles y asclepias aquí.

LACED BOUQUETS
RAMOS DE ENCAJE O ENTRELAZADO

Face Forward
De un solo frente

A rectangular vase works well as the container for a one-sided laced bouquet, a gently sloping wall of flowers including sunflower buds, gerberas, dahlias, and kangaroo paws. The edges of the vase support the first stem placements, which in turn support others, allowing for a tapestry of flower forms and colors, like a carpet being lifted up to show its pattern.

Una base rectangular funciona bien para contener un ramo entrelazado, de un solo frente, produciendo un gentil montículo. Incluye botones de girasol, gerberas, dalias y patas de canguro. La orilla de la base es soporte de los primeros tallos que, a su vez, son soporte de otros, creando un tapiz de formas y colores, parecido a una alfombra levantada para mostrar su diseño.

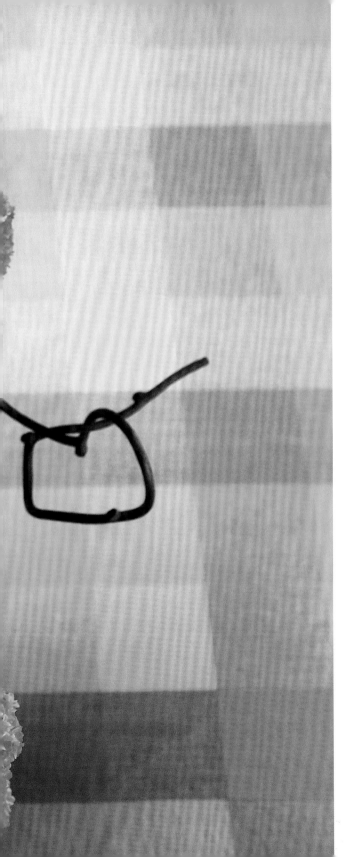

ARMATURE BOUQUETS
RAMOS ARMAZÓN

Support System   Sistema de soporte

Sturdy, woody, horizontal stems can be used to support softer, vertical flower stems in a variety of ways that give you control over the shape and density of the completed bouquet. An armature can be any supportive framework. This kiwi-vine grid is an elementary example. It simply rests on top of the vase, and the stems of green viburnum and blue hydrangea are inserted through it. The left side of the composite photo shows the grid alone, the right side one-half of the completed bouquet.

De madera y resistentes, los tallos horizontales dan soporte a flores y tallos suaves y verticales y, de diversos modos, permiten mayor control sobre la forma y densidad del acabado del ramo. Un armazón es cualquier estructura de soporte. Este enrejado hecho de ramas de kiwi sirve de ejemplo básico.

Solamente descansa sobre el jarrón, mientras los tallos de viburnum verde e hydrangea azul le son agregados. El lado izquierdo de este conjunto fotográfico muestra la cuadrícula sola; el derecho, una mitad del arreglo terminado.

Vine, Twigs, Grasses
Ramas, ramillas y hierbas

An armature might be as simple as one long piece of ivy vine, stripped of all but a few leaves, and wound round and round into a flat spiral. To hold the loops of vine in place, weave wrapped wire through them. Attach sturdy, straight branches to the disk of looped vine in three places with more wrapped wire, so the branches extend below to form the outline of the bouquet. Add bear grass, weaving some of it through the loops of vine. Finally, insert flower and more foliage stems through the armature, slanting them toward the binding point at the center.

Un armazón es tan simple como un gran retazo de hiedra, sin hojas, salvo algunas, y acomodada en círculos, bien redondos, cual espiral plana. Para sostener los círculos, es necesario pasar un alambre entre ellos. Se deben agregar ramas resistentes al disco obtenido, en tres lugares, con más adhesiones de alambre forrado, de modo que las ramas se extiendan, hacia abajo, haciendo el trazo del ramo. Agregue salvia, tejiendo sus hojas entre los círculos del armazón. Finalmente, inserte flores y más tallos, de pocas hojas, a través del armazón, doblándolos a modo de formar un punto de unión, en el centro.

Less Is More

Menos es más

Here, trimming and pruning yields a dark, dramatic bouquet. The stem-absorbed dye that turns the sunflower petals orange also turns the center and the sepals a rich purple. Remove the petals and the purple comes to the fore. Likewise, the leaves are removed from cherry branches, which are then bundled and bent into an oval armature, using paper-wrapped wire to hold the shape. Flower and foliage stems are inserted through the armature into the oval vase. Lavender flowers are just the right color if the leaves and topmost petals are removed.

Aquí, recortar y podar resulta en un ramo dramático y oscuro. El teñido penetra los tallos volviendo anaranjados los pétalos de un girasol y el centro y los sépalos verdes del cáliz, morado profundo. Remueva los pétalos y el morado resaltará más. Quite las hojas de las ramas de cerezo y póngalas en manojo dándoles forma oval. Se utiliza alambre forrado para fijar la forma. Las flores y el follaje se insertan a través del armazón en un jarrón también oval. Las flores lavanda son el color perfecto, si se elimina sus pétalos de más arriba.

Swirling Green Espiral de verdes

Nasturtium vine, with leaves and flowers removed, provides a sturdy yet flexible armature material. Try holding a few stems of the vine at the bottom and winding the long tops around each other, then tucking them in to approximate the shape of a bouquet. As you add flower stems (here, roses, gerberas, and larkspur, along with green euphorbia and bupleurum) the fresh vine may loosen. Let it. Bound and placed in a green vase, the bouquet is enhanced by the softly swirling, swagged loops of vine.

The fresh light green is also picked up by the outer petals of the roses, which have been bred for this decorative feature, so don't mistake the green petals for sepals or "guard petals" and remove them.

Una rama de nasturtium, ya sin hojas ni flores, sirve de armazón, resistente y flexible a la vez. Pruebe a sostener varios de los tallos de su rama creando un fondo y dando forma a sus puntas, rodeándose unas a otras, unidas, hasta dar la forma deseada. A medida en que agrega flores de tallo (rosas, gerberas, consolida, euphrobia verde y bupleurum) su rama, aún fresca, dará de sí. Déjela. Unido y colocado el armazón en un jarrón verde, el ramo se embellecerá gracias a los espirales y vueltas obtenidas con la viña.

El fresco verde claro también será realzado por los pétalos exteriores de las rosas, cultivados para esta función decorativa. Usted no debe confundir ni eliminar los pétalos verdes con los estambres del cáliz.

Curves Ahead

Curvas al frente

Fresh cape honeysuckle vines, part woody, part green, with most of the foliage removed, are easily fashioned into an organic, intriguingly textured armature. The long, lovely stems of the tulips are shaped in graceful curves by pulling the blooms back in toward the center of the bouquet and tying the stems to the armature with paper-wrapped wire. The cut tulips will continue to grow, stretching and turning and adding to the interest of the bouquet.

Las ramas de madreselva fresca, en parte de madera, en parte verdes y libres de casi todo su follaje, son fácilmente moldeables para formar un armazón orgánico, de texturas fascinantes. Los largos y encantadores tallos de los tulipanes son acomodados en graciosas curvas, colocados mirando hacia el centro del ramo, fijos sus tallos al armazón, con ayuda de alambre forrado. Los tulipanes, ya cortados, continuarán creciendo, estirándose y girando para, de ese modo, añadir interés a este arreglo.

Pure Lilac Pureza de lila

Lilac stems make a romantic choice for a bridal bouquet—but lilacs are among those tender flowers that will not last out of water even as long as it takes to carry them down the aisle. For those who love lilacs, and the look of a hand-tied bouquet, there is a solution: the faux hand-tied, in which the flowers drink from floral foam in a hidden bouquet holder.

Lilacs, like other woody stems, are heavy drinkers that require a bouquet holder with a large foam cage.

For this bouquet, the holder's white plastic handle was covered with brown floral tape, and leaves glued to the underside of the cage with floral adhesive. Lilac stems cover the handle, secured with paper-wrapped wire. The cut end of a long piece of asparagus fern is inserted into the foam, the fern is wound around the cage, and the tip is pinned to the foam with a snippet of chenille stem, which swells in the foam and lodges securely.

Las lilas son románticas para un ramo de novia—pero se cuentan entre las flores tiernas que no vivirán, fuera del agua, ni lo que tome llegar al altar. Para aquellos que adoran las lilas y la apariencia de un ramo de mano, hay solución: el falso atado en que las flores beben de una espuma floral, oculta en el mango del ramo.

Al igual que otros tallos de madera, las lilas requieren mucha agua y un contenedor grande de espuma. Se debe

envolver cinta floral alrededor del mango plástico blanco y usar pegamento de flores para adherir las hojas a su parte inferior. Al final se aseguran los extremos de las lilas, al mango, con alambre forrado. Una pieza larga de helecho de espárrago cubrirá la espuma. Inserte en ella las puntas cortadas. Dé varias vueltas al helecho alrededor del contenedor y asegure con un alfiler la punta a la espuma, agregando un pedacito de chenille que, al ensancharse, servirá de cuña.

Stem Anchors Cuñas para los tallos

Two things lend realism to a faux hand-tied bouquet made in a bouquet holder: one is covering the plastic handle with sections of real cut stems. The other is the way you insert the flowers into the foam. Because you want to work a lot of flowers into a small amount of foam, it's helpful to use chenille stems whenever possible. Insert one end of a length of chenille stem into the flower stem, the other into the bouquet holder. The chenille wicks moisture efficiently from the foam to the flower, while the wire at its core provides control, holds securely, and takes up very little room in the foam. In this bouquet all the flowers except the thin-stemmed jasmine are equipped with chenille inserts.

Dos cosas vuelven realista un ramo artificialmente unido a un contenedor: una es que quede cubierto el mango plástico, con cortes de tallo vivos. La otra es el modo en que inserte las flores a la base de espuma. Como pondrá un montón de flores sobre una espuma más bien pequeña, ayúdese con tallos de chenille donde pueda. Inserte una punta del chenille a sus flores y otra al contenedor. El chenille transportará la humedad, eficientemente, de la espuma a la flor; su estructura de alambre controlará y asegurará el arreglo, ocupando poco espacio en la espuma. En este ramo todas las flores, menos las de tallos más delgados, como el jazmín, llevan una cuña de chenille.

Let's Pretend Hagamos de cuenta

Using the real stems of peony tulips and viburnum to cover the bouquet holder handle makes this "hand-tied bouquet" a convincing fake. Ribbon covers the rubber band that holds the stems onto the handle; repeated knots of ribbon add a decorative detail. Chenille inserts allow compact placement of the peony tulips; the woody stems of viburnum are inserted directly into the foam. For an even better grip, small pieces of chenille stem may be attached to woody stems like viburnum or lilac using floral tape. Both the natural and the chenille stem should penetrate the foam.

Utilizar tallos reales de tulipán y hoja de maple, para cubrir el mango, hace más convincente este falso ramo. El listón cubre la liga que une a los tallos, formando el mango; los nudos del listón agregan un detalle decorativo. Inserciones de chenille permiten colocar, en forma compacta, los tulipanes; los tallos de maple se insertan directamente en la espuma. Pequeñas cuñas de chenille se adhieren a la madera del tallo, de maple o de lila, con la ayuda de cinta floral, para asegurarlos. Tanto los tallos naturales como el chenille se insertan en la espuma floral.

Finishing Touches

Últimos toques

The underside of a faux hand-tied bouquet, where the handle meets the flowers, is critical to the illusion. A foliage collar or "doily," layered on top of the foam cage and its stem-covered handle, adds realism along with classic decorative detail. Here are two alternatives for finishing a bouquet of frilly cottage tulips. In each case, the foliage stems, still attached, mingle with the cut tulip stems.

La parte inferior del falso ramo, donde se unen flores y mango, es critica para crear ilusión. Un anillo o adorno colocado sobre la espuma y el mango cubierto de tallos añade realismo y un detalle decorativo clásico. A continuación, dos alternativas para dar los toques finales a un ramo de dinámicos tulipanes. En cada caso, el follaje, todavía adherido, se conjuga con los tallos cortados de tulipán.

Criss-Cross Cruzado

Hand-tied bouquets aren't the only way to arrange flowers that's easy, natural, and allows them to drink directly from water mixed with flower-food in the vase. Of the many ways to create a grid across the top of a vase, using ribbon has the advantage of decorating the vase itself. Stems inserted between the strips of ribbon can be positioned as you please.

Los ramos de mano no son la única manera, sencilla y natural, de arreglar las flores y que éstas beban de un contenedor con alimento. De entre muchas maneras de crear una cuadrícula, para colocarla sobre el borde de un jarrón, usar listón ofrece la ventaja de decorar el jarrón también. Los tallos se insertan en la cuadrícula y se acomodan al gusto.

ALTERNATIVE STRATEGIES

ESTRATEGIAS ALTERNATIVAS

Disappearing Act
Acto de magia

Narrow, clear plastic floral tape can be used to form a disappearing grid. The ends of the tape should just grip the rim of the bowl. With a combination like these light-green grasses and deep-purple anemones and sweetpeas, it's easier to begin by adding the grasses to the center sections of the grid, fanning out in all directions. Then place the flowers, working from the outside in. The stems of the outer blooms can provide additional support for those at the center, which should rise a little higher for a mounded effect. Add more grasses, if needed, for the perfect blend.

Cinta adhesiva invisible, angosta, sirve para formar una rejilla, que desaparecerá. Las puntas de la cinta se fijan, apenas, al borde de la base. Una combinación de pastos, en verde claro, y anémonas de morado profundo con flor de chícharo hacen fácil agregar el verde desde el centro, ampliándose en forma de abanico, en todas direcciones. Coloque anémonas, de afuera hacia adentro. Tallos y brotes exteriores proveen soporte adicional para las flores del centro, que se elevan sobre el resto, dando un efecto de montículo. Agregue hierbas, donde sea necesario, hasta dar con la mezcla perfecta.

Cool, Calm, Collected

Fresco, tranquilo y sereno

Collections of small, individual vases with narrow necks make it easy to control flowers and give them plenty to drink. An assembly of such vases often makes a unified impression even when they are not physically linked, but it may add to the impact of the design if you choose to do so. Cymbidium sprays, fresh honeysuckle vine, and bear grass, for example, can create soothing horizontal lines, a pleasing variation on the usual array of upright stems. Here two stems of cymbidiums were cut and divided among the three vases.

Conjuntos de floreros, individuales, pequeños, de cuello angosto, procuran mayor control de las flores y sirven para darles de beber. Un conjunto así, produce con frecuencia un efecto de unidad, aún cuando los floreros no estén físicamente unidos. Colocarlos así agrega impacto al diseño que se elije. Brotes de cymbidium, tiras frescas de madreselva, y ramas de salvia, por ejemplo, crean líneas horizontales, produciendo un placentero contraste con la acostumbrada verticalidad de los tallos. Aquí, dos tallos de cymbidium son cortados y divididos en tres floreros.

All About Accessories
Todo acerca de los accesorios

Repetition is the key to a pleasing collection of single blooms. Simple accents, also repeated, can power-fully enhance the effect. At far left, the hard beauty of the shells dramatizes the soft peach of the gerberas; to emphasize the shells, some vases are left without flowers. A single aspidistra leaf is wrapped around each of the taller gerberas in a two-level display. At near left, red dogwood twigs, in the vase and on the table, pull a collection of cymbidium bud vases together as a decorative unit. The twigs support the cymbidium blooms upright and pull out the darker color of the orchid lips.

La repetición es clave en esta agradable colección de botones. Los acentos sencillos ven aumentado su impacto al repetirse. En el extremo izquierdo, la belleza recia de las conchas añade dramatismo, contrastando con el suave color durazno de las gerberas. Algunos jarrones se dejan sin flores para realzar a las conchas. Una hoja solitaria de aspidistra envuelve a cada gerberas altas, propiciando dos niveles. En el interior izqui-erdo, ramas de cerezo, en jarrón y mesa, realzan la colección de brotes de cymbidium, puestos en unidad decorativa; las ramas les sirven de marco y sacan a relucir, también, el color más oscuro de las orquídeas (orquid labellum).

Lily White *Puro blanco*

With their large, outward-facing blooms and branching stems, Oriental lilies are a natural choice for display as multiples. Single stems placed in individual vases have a combined impact that is greater than the sum of its parts. Wrapping the necks of the vases with wrapped wire, twine, or a similar material adds textural contrast.

Las lilas orientales, con sus grandes brotes y ramas mirando hacia afuera, se dan a elegir naturalmente en presentaciones múltiples. Sus solitarios tallos, colocados en jarrones individuales, producen un impacto combinado mayor que la suma de sus partes. El envolver los cuellos de los jarrones de alambre forrado, ramas o material similar, añade textura contrastante.

The Blues   Los azules

Small hand-tied bouquets are also effective as multiples. These cord-wrapped vases come in three related colors. Each color finds an echo in the flowers chosen for the nosegays, a combination of mass (perennial scabiosa) and form flowers (campanula and iris) in various shades of blue.

Los ramos de mano pequeños son efectivos si múltiples. Estas bases, envueltas con cordón, vienen en tres colores afines. Cada color hace eco de las flores elegidas para los ramilletes, combinando volumen (perennial scabiosa) y forma (campanula e iris), en diversos tonos de azul.

Color Story
Un cuento de color

In the European tradition of hand-tied bouquets, the wrapping is essential, especially when the bouquet is a gift. It's not only a matter of protecting the bouquet as it travels from the flower shop to the home. A beautiful presentation enhances its value. The selection of wrapping materials and the technique of wrapping offer another opportunity for high craft and creativity. Color matching or contrast is an important part of this story. A well-chosen floral wrap can lend a smaller bouquet a feeling of substance.

En la tradición europea de los ramos de mano la envoltura es esencial, especialmente si el ramo es un regalo. No se trata sólo de proteger el ramo en su trayecto, de la florería a la casa. Una bella presentación, realza su valor. Escoger los materiales y la técnica de la envoltura da pie a la creatividad y al alto oficio. Combinar colores o contrastarlos es importante en este cuento. Una envoltura floral, bien elegida, agrega a un ramo pequeño, sensación de sustancia.

All Dressed Up

Bien vestidos

Cellophane, plastic wrap, and ribbon can all play a decorative as well as functional role. Two colors of wrap, orange and hot pink, make the vivid hues of this generously wrapped bouquet pop. Clear cellophane outside the tissue adds reflective sheen, retains moisture, and protects the stem ends. Ribbon can be used on its own or to cover a rubber band. Proportionally adjusted, the same wrap can serve as an accent to the bouquet in the vase.

El celofán, la envoltura plástica y el listón tienen un rol decorativo y funcional a la vez. Los dos colores, naranja y rosa encendido, aportan tonos vivos, al ramito, generosamente envuelto. El celofán transparente, agrega cierto reflejo brillante, al tiempo que retiene la humedad y protege las puntas de los tallos. El listón se usa solo o sobre una liga. La misma envoltura, proporcionalmente ajustada, sirve de acento al ramo, ya en el jarrón.

Classic Chrysanthemum

Clásico de crisantemos

A classic European hand-tied bouquet gets the classic wrapping treatment of cellophane and plastic wrap. The bouquet celebrates the Oriental opulence of large white chrysanthemums, of the type affectionately known in America as football mums, and the wrapping underscores their shape and color with an echo, writ large—just as the tiny white matricaria flowers echo them in miniature. In the home, the wrapping is replaced with a white vase.

Un ramo europeo clásico lleva envoltura de celofán o plástico, también clásica. El arreglo celebra la opulencia oriental de los enormes crisantemos blancos, del tipo que en Estados Unidos se nombra afectuosamente balones de fútbol. La envoltura subraya la forma y el color, a manera de imitación, en grande—al igual que las diminutas y blancas matricarias que le hacen eco. En casa, la envoltura es remplazada por un jarrón blanco.

Sophisticated Simplicity

Sofisticada simplicidad

The simplest of wrappings—in this case, clear cellophane—can be embellished in a manner worthy of the contents. Tied off with strands of curled paper-wrapped wire and accented with brown galax leaves, the bouquet combines ranunculus and burgundy callas with ornamental mini pineapples, sunflower centers, and assorted foliage.

In the home, the wrapping comes off, and on the next two pages, we see the elements of the same bouquet distributed among three similar vases for a linked, rhythmic effect.

La simpleza de las envolturas—en el caso del celofán transparente—puede embellecer considerablemente sus contenidos. Atado con tiras de papel rizado, alambre forrado y hojas de lotus cafés, el ramo combina ranunculus y callas borgoñas con adornos de pequeñas piñas, centros de girasol y follaje de varios tipos.

En casa, la envoltura se quita y, como lo vemos en las próximas dos páginas, elementos del mismo ramo se distribuyen en tres jarrones similares, dando un efecto rítmico de unidad.

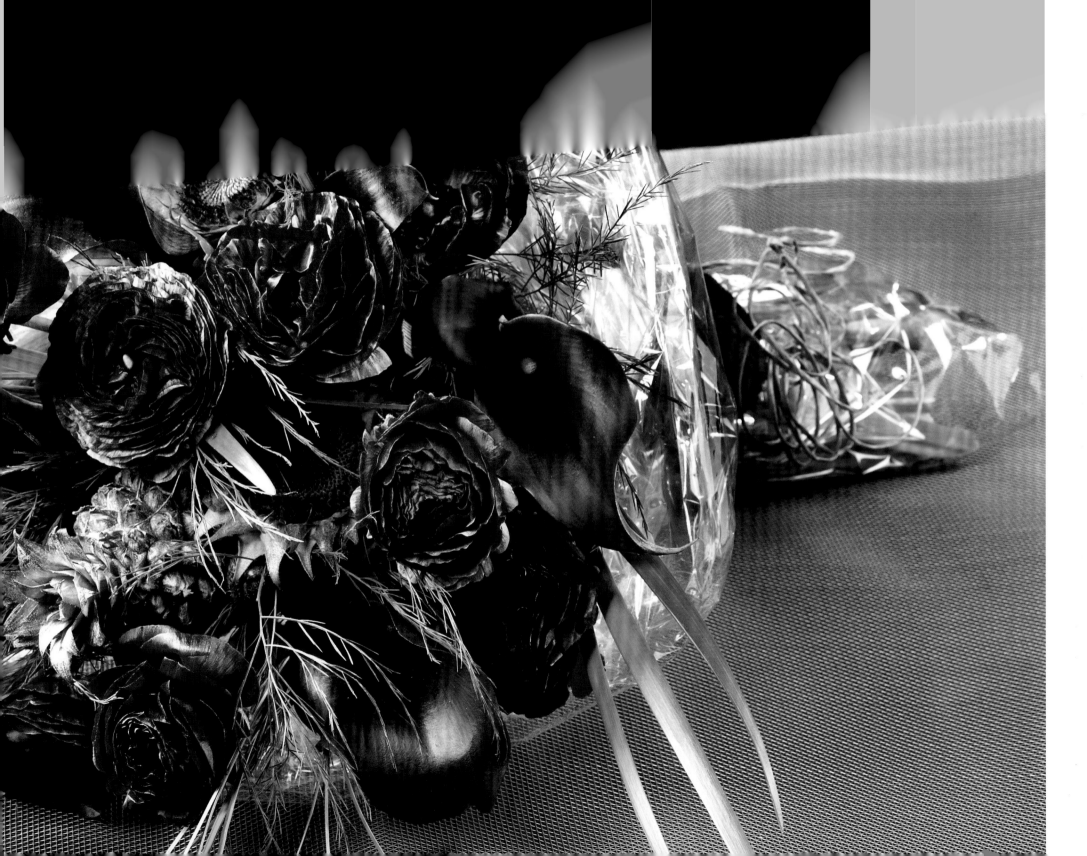

Silver Screen

Malla plateada

Aluminum wire mesh (window screen), with the edges crimped to prevent scratches, complements an all-white bouquet with its neutral sheen. (White wrapping paper, even off-white or ivory, would have a very different effect.) In the home, a pot with a rim of matte metal serves similarly as a color complement to the white flowers and gray-green foliage.

Malla de alambre (de ventana), con las puntas dobladas para evitar rasguños, se suma bien al ramo, todo blanco, con brillo neutral. (Papel blanco, crema o marfil, da al conjunto un efecto distinto.) En casa, una maceta de borde metálico mate sirve de complemento al blanco de las flores y al verde grisáceo del follaje.

To Give, To Enjoy

Dar y disfrutar

Lavender wrap brings out the accent color in a finely textured bouquet, while an inner layer of fiber mesh complements the gray-green tones and feathery frills of fillers and foliage.

Envoltura lavanda acentúa el color y la fina textura de este ramo. Una capa interior de malla de fibra complementa los tonos verde grisáceo y el ligero movimiento de las hojas de relleno.

Fresh and Dried

Fresco y seco

Preserved lotus leaves make an exotic wrapping for 'Mambo' spray roses. By wrapping an inner bouquet, adding more roses, and rewrapping with more lotus leaves, an effect of segmentation is created on the top surface of the bouquet. A bundle of ivy vine, stripped of nearly all its leaves, holds the outermost wrapping in place and supports the tall sheaf of roses.

Las hojas de un lotus, preservadas, son envoltura exótica de un manojo de rosas mambo. Cubrir un ramo interior e ir agregando rosas y, luego, otra envoltura de lotus, da efecto de segmentación a la superficie. Una tira de hiedra, casi sin hojas, mantiene la envoltura exterior en su lugar y da soporte al conjunto más alto de rosas.

Green Sheath

Envueltos de verde

Daisies, strawflowers, and their miniature counterparts, ammobium flowers, have a sunny, informal character. These rustic beauties are adapted to to the drawing-room, however, with a dramatic wrapping of broad green anthurium leaves (held in place with double-faced tape) that lends a touch of chic. It's our final demonstration of how the bouquet-maker's art, observant and respectful of nature, celebrates style.

Margaritas, siemprevivas, y flores de ammobium—sus contrapartes en miniatura—, son luminosas e informales. Bellezas rústicas, adaptadas al cuarto de dibujo, envueltas en hoja ancha y verde de anthurium (sostenidas con cinta de doble lado) dan el toque de elegancia. Ésta es nuestra demostración final de cómo el arte de hacer ramos, observador y respetuoso de la naturaleza, celebra el estilo.

Mass Flower Identification

1. Hypericum androsaemum/ coffee bean berry
2. Rosa hybrid 'Milva'/hybrid Tea rose
3. Hydrangea macrophilla/ hydrangea
4. Tulipa hybrid/tulip
5. Narcissus species/daffodil
6. Tulipa hybrid/"French" tulip
7. Brassica oleracea/ornamental cabbage

8. Dianthus caryophyllus/ carnation
9. Gerbera jamesonii/gerbera daisy
10. Dianthus caryophyllus/spray carnation
11. Chrysanthemum indicum/ football mum
12. Helianthus annuus/sunflower
13. Echinacea purpurea/cone flower (plucked)

14. Hydrangea macrophilla/ hydrangea
15. Ranunculus asiaticus/Persian ranunculus
16. Gerbera jamesonii/gerbera daisy
17. Eustoma grandiflorum/ lisianthus
18. Dahlia hybrid/dahlia
19. Helianthus annuus 'Teddy Bear'/teddy bear sunflower

20. Rosa hybrid/hybrid Tea rose
21. Alstroemeria species
22. Chrysanthymum indicum 'Inga'/standard mum
23. Helianthus annuus 'Indian Summer'/Indian summer sunflower
24. Scabiosa caucasica/pincushion flower
25. see Scabiosa caucasica
26. Anemone coronaria/wind flower

27. Ranunculus asiaticus/Persian ranunculus
28. Chrysanthemum indicum 'Statesman'/spray mum
29. Paeonia lactiflora/peony
30. Rosa hybrid 'Macarena'/spray rose
31. Syringa vulgaris/lilac
32. Dianthus caryophyllus/ carnation
33. Gerbera jamesonii/gerbera daisy

34. Chrysanthemum indicum 'Yoko Ono'/spray mum
35. Rosa hybrid 'Freedom'/Hybrid tea rose
36. Chrysanthemum frutescens/ marguerite daisy
37. Helianthus annuus 'Sunbright'/ sunflower
38. Rosa hybrid 'Supernova'/spray rose
39. Craspedia globosa/billy buttons

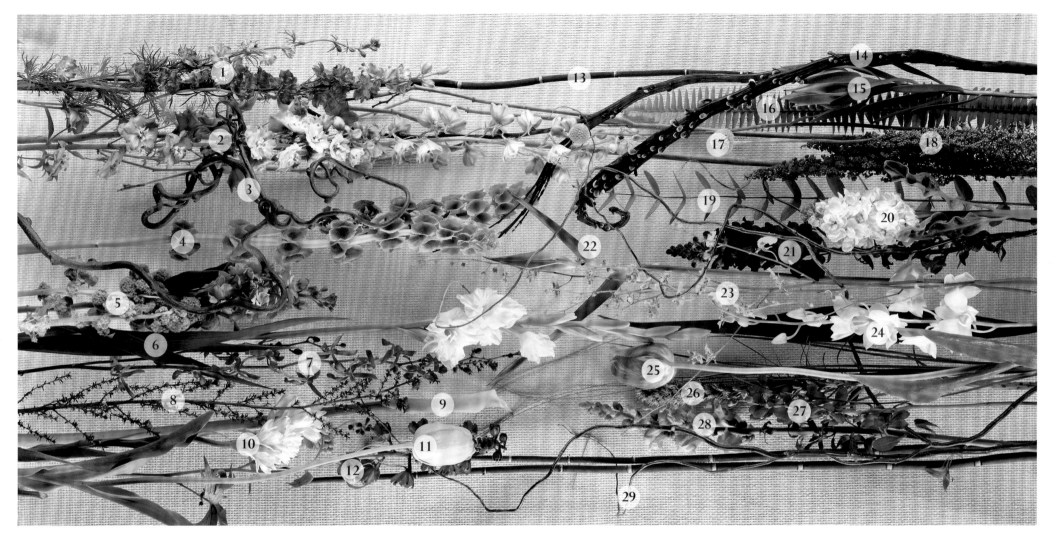

Line Flower Identification

1. Delphinium ajacis/larkspur
2. Delphinium elatum/hybrid delphinium
3. Actinidia chinensis/kiwi vine
4. Moluccella laevis/bells of Ireland
5. Amaranthus species/tassle flower

6. Gladiolus hybride/gladiolus
7. Aragnus species/orchid
8. Leptospermum scoparium/ blue lepto
9. Zantedeschia aethiopica/calla lily
10. Polianthes tuberosa/tuberose
11. Tulipa hybride "Apricot"/ "French" tulip

12. Delphinium "Belladonna Group"/delphinium
13. Equisetum hyemale/horsetail
14. Salix udensis 'Sekka'/ fantail willow
15. Leucodendron species/ leucadendron
16. Nephrolepis cordifolia/sword fern

17. Craspedia globosa/Billy buttons
18. Erica persoluta/heather
19. Eucalyptus species/gum/"euc"
20. Matthiola incana/stock
21. Anthirrinum majus/ snapdragon
22. Heliconia psittacorum/ parakeet heliconia

23. Oncidium species/ popcorn orchid
24. Dendrobium species/ dendrobium orchid
25. Tulipa hybride/"French" tulip
26. Liatris spicata/gay feather
27. Anthirrinum majus/ snapdragon

28. Anthirrinum majus/ snapdragon
29. Salix mutsudana 'Tortuosa'/ curly willow

Filler Flower Identification

1. Athenum graveolens/dill
2. Thalictrum dipterocarpum/ meadow rue
3. Limonium sinuatum/statice
4. Solidago hybride/goldenrod

5. Limonum perezii/seafoam statice
6. Tanacetum parthenium/ feverfew
7. Agonis hybride/peppermint tree

8. Heteromeles arbutifolia/ California Holly
9. Gypsophila paniculata/baby's breath
10. Limonium sinuatum/statice

11. Achillea millefolium/cottage yarrow
12. Linum usitatissimum/flax seed
13. Leptospermum rotundifolium/ blue lepto

14. Aster Novi-Belgii/monte casino aster
15. Ammi visnaga/green mist
16. Chamelaucium pheliferum/ waxflower

17. Bupleurum rotundifolium/ thoroughwax
18. Gypsophila paniculata 'Million Stars'/gyp
19. Chamelaucium hybride/New Zealand waxflower

Form Flower Identification

1. Lilium Hybrid Con'Amore/ Oriental lily
2. Heliconia caribaea/lobster claw
3. Banksia ashbyi/banksia
4. Iris Hollandica 'Telstar'/Dutch Iris
5. Anthurium andreanum/ Anthurium
6. Heliconia psittacorum 'Parakeet'/Parakeet heliconia

7. Gloriosa rothschildiana/ Rothchild lily
8. Guzmania species/bromeliad flower
9. Anigozanthos flavidus/ kangeroo paw
10. Leucospermum reflexum/ pincushion protea
11. Nelumbo nucifera/lotus pod
12. Anthurium species/anthurium

13. Protea magnifica/Queen protea
14. Hyacinthus orientalis/hyacinth
15. Strelitzia reginae/bird of paradise
16. Leucodendron discolor/ leucodendron
17. Lilium orientalis 'Stargazer'/ Oriental lily
18. Alpinia purpurata/ginger

19. Ananas spectabilis/ornamental pineapple
20. Protea cynaroides/king protea
21. Curcuma domestica/olena
22. Leucospermum nutans/ pincusion protea
23. Phalaenopsis amabilis/moth orchid
24. Calathea crotalifera/rattlesnake flower

25. Zantedeschia species/mini calla
26. Cymbidium hybrid/miniature cymbidium orchid
27. Zingiber spectabile/golden beehive ginger
28. Scilla species/scilla
29. Freesia hybrid/Freesia
30. Narcissus 'Grand Soleil d'Or'/ narcissus

31. Pahiopedilum leeanum/lady slipper orchid
32. Protea nerifolia/sugarbush protea
33. Cattleya hybrid/cattleya orchid
34. Zantedeschia aetiopica/calla lily
35. Brunia albiflora

Twigs, Berries, Buds, and Pods Identification

1. Equisetum hyemale/horsetail
2. Aparagus plumosus vine/plumosus
3. Physalis species fruit/Chinese latern
4. Pennisetum glaucum 'Purple Majesty'/millet
5. Rumex crispus/dock
6. Monarda species/bee balm
7. Sabal mexicana/palmetto palm date frond
8. Crocosmia crocosmiliiflora/montbretia pods
9. Viburnum opulus/viburnum berries
10. Pyracantha coccinea/firethorn berries
11. Pittosporum species/pittosporum with fruit
12. Helichrysum species/curry
13. Helenium bigelovii/sneezewind
14. Pitrus juncus/rush
15. Eucalyptus species/eucaluptus flower buds
16. Platanus racemosa/sycamore seed clusters
17. Typha latifolia/cattail foliage
18. Ananas comosus species/ornamental mini pineapple
19. Papaver nudicaule/Iceland poppy buds
20. Helilanthus annuus/sunflower plucked disk
21. Palmetto species/Palmetto palm dates
22. Prunus persica/immature peach fruit
23. Nelumbo nucifera/lotus pod
24. Pinus albicaulis/immature pine cone
25. Papaver orientale/opium poppy pods
26. Briza maxima/rattlesnake grass
27. Arum italicum/seed cluster
28. Ligustrum vulgare/privet berry
29. Setaria italica/millet
30. Ficus species/edible fig

ABOUT RENÉ VAN REMS

René van Rems is a world-renowned ambassador of the floral industry.

Originally from Amsterdam, The Netherlands, René has called San Diego, California, home for over 20 years. He is a member of the American Institute of Floral Designers (AIFD), The National Speakers Association, and the Professional Floral Commentators International (PFCI).

René was formally educated in the entire spectrum of Floriculture/Horticulture through his studies at the Rijksmiddelbare Tuinbouwschool at Aalsmeer (Floral Institute). He has led design shows, workshops, and seminars throughout the US, Canada, Europe, and Asia on the styling of fresh-cut flowers.

A frequent speaker at leading art museums including the Minneapolis Art Institute and San Francisco's de Young Museum, René has also been featured in numerous national publications like *California Florists*, *Sunset* Magazine, *Flowers &* Magazine, *Floral Management*, *Florist* Magazine, and *Flower News*. René's design work has been featured in *Better Homes & Gardens* as well as the *Florists' Review* publication of 101 Wedding Bouquets.

René and his work have been covered on television (HGTV), particularly for his European influence on trends in American floral design. In 1995, the American Horticultural Society awarded him the Francis Jones Poetker Award, and in 2001, Van Rems was the recipient of the Los Angeles Flower Market's first annual René van Rems Award for excellence in design education.

René served ten years as Director of Promotion for the California Cut Flower Commission.

Dear René,

Thank you so much for the delightful day you gave the Pasadena Garden Club. You had the ladies laughing from the beginning to the end. Everyone went home with a smile on their face. Your program was entertaining, enlightening and beautiful to watch. We all learned a lot about flower arranging and the care and treatment of cut flowers. The arrangements you made were amazing and six lucky ladies are still enjoying the fruits of the day. I would be happy to recommend you to any group for a great speaker. It is so difficult to find a speaker of your caliber, groups are always looking for people like you. You educated us, you made us laugh, you are easy on the eyes so the ladies all like that, and you have such a store of knowledge to share. You have made me look REALLY good as Program Director. Wow! It was great fun. Thank you for agreeing to come to Pasadena and share your many gifts with us.

Sincerely,
Kathy Dooling
Program Director
Pasadena Garden Club

Dear René,

I write to thank you for your gracious participation in Art Alive 2005 and for your continued dedication to SDMA's signature event. As you know already, Art Alive is the major fundraising emphasis for the San Diego Museum of Art and this year it exceeded many of our expectations.

Over the years you have provided unparalleled support and enthusiasm for Art Alive through a variety of measures. This year's rotunda design was bold and innovative, sparking the imaginations of more than 9,000 visitors. Another highlight was your "Flower Power" Iron Chef-style floral demonstration in 2003. This presentation truly revealed your dynamic personality, helped forge important relationships with other leading floral designers, and unquestionably "wowed" the crowd.

Thanks to you, we also re-invigorated the floral demonstration/lecture program for 2005, to the delight of many floral enthusiasts. SDMA is proud to affiliate with René van Rems International, and I can honestly say that you are one of my most cherished community partners. I send you my heartfelt thanks and very best wishes.

Sincerely,
Sarah E. Beckman
Senior Development Manager
San Diego Musem of Art